Sappho Prompts

poems by

Margaret Lee

Finishing Line Press
Georgetown, Kentucky

Sappho Prompts

Copyright © 2026 by Margaret Lee
ISBN 979-8-89990-303-8 First Edition
All rights reserved under International and Pan-American Copyright Conventions. No part of this book may be reproduced in any manner whatsoever without written permission from the publisher, except in the case of brief quotations embodied in critical articles and reviews.

Publisher: Leah Huete de Maines
Editor: Christen Kincaid
Cover Art: Margaret Lee
Author Photo: Margaret Lee
Cover Design: Elizabeth Maines McCleavy

Order online: www.finishinglinepress.com
also available on amazon.com

Author inquiries and mail orders:
Finishing Line Press
PO Box 1626
Georgetown, Kentucky 40324
USA

Contents

Water Song for Sappho 1

Melody
Someone Else's Earth 5
Entwined 6

This edgeless birthing 7
Unbounded 9
Ode to Artemis 10
Becoming "I" 11
Consuming Tide 12
Sense of Change 13
Ever-Weeping Rock 14
Desert Litany 15
On Beginning Again 16

False boundary of the body 17
The Space Between 19
Confrontation 20
Love Song 21
Intermingled 22
Bird-Sisters 23
Unwelcome Visitors 26
In Parallel 27
Love Nest 28

Bridge
Unhinged 31
Cosmogenesis 32

A hue this side of dark 33
To Sappho 35
Petronia petronia 36
Earthbound 37
Iokolpos 38
Ground Cover 39
Precipice 40
Hope 41

Waiting river 43
Thumos 45

What Waits for Me	46
Seascape	47
Stalagmos	48
Unraveled	49
In the Air	50
Acheron	51
Still Life with Doves	53

Coda

Cento Duet	57
Prayer	58

Meet Sappho 59

Notes 63

Fragment Index 71

Artist's Statement 75

Acknowledgments 76

For Brandon,

Aphrodite's answer

(Chorus):
Called *Poetess* in ancient times,
her fragments lost, then found,
papyrus scraps preserve her voice,
her artistry unbound.

Water Song for Sappho

Become my voice.

```
        lyrics
Your        rode              currents
                memory
```

```
then
    settled
            in the pith
                    of green
```

```
papyrus sprung
            from river waters
                        of your island home
                    flowing into
        my inner well.
```

```
I dive
    for
        missing pieces.
```

Melody

Someone Else's Earth

*Stars around the lovely moon
hold back
their brilliant shape.*
We are ever
someone else's earth,
a poem unwritten.

I exist, not
I, but *poiesis*—
a woman changing.

*Just now,
Gold-sandaled Dawn*
set her footprint
on the indigo horizon,

a poet's canvas.

My inner fire—
what I don't know
I know.

My *thought*
a creaking hinge,
pale light—the moment

insight steps barefoot
through the clutter, a child
when no one else is awake.

I taste it like *cold water*—
finding,
being found.

Entwined

Lip of being,
        woven plentitude,
                spangled Earth!

Our planet's molten core births the limestone web
of former seas, silica-flecks of old volcano blasts,
the plaited geosphere—

and I, *Wordweaver*, love the Earth by noticing
the lanky prairie grasses twined with wildflowers,
by naming russet bison, candescent fire,

bleached bones, all in motion to dust, the ashy
smolder that unfolds again as seal or snowy owl,
its ice-crust realm—the braided biome.

Speech-strands spun into the running twist
catch Star River specks, etching bare tree limbs
against blue foothills, a lustrous yarn

plied smooth. Spendthrift, I lavish my attention
on the journey of Becoming, twin to Absence.
Speech-spinner, song braider, in thrall,

I name this moment.

This edgeless birthing

(Chorus):
The woven threads of destiny
entangle broken strands.
Their interlacement builds a story
told with artful hands.

Unbounded

I used to braid crowns of emerald tendrils,
      amethyst blossoms.
Sweet clover and I
      ran wild in summer.

Our leggy stems escaped
the mower's slash
where severed grass bled green,
its crisp bouquet choked
by engine fumes.

I fled beyond
the sidewalk's concrete rim
      to clover-studded fields—
           uncut grass
   swayed
        fragrant,
             baking sunshine.

White blossoms blushing pink,
      tiny trumpet clusters.
I twined their stems
      plucked slim florets
           squeezed the rosy base
                between my teeth—
       quick, sweet flush!

Garlands
      bracelets
           headbands—

my unbounded world.

Ode to Artemis

Shout down
the father-god, the whole
sky!

By your head, you swore,
I will forever
 remain unowned,
  unbroken
 on lonely mountaintops,
  hunting.

Barefoot on mountain peaks
you stood your ground
alone, toned for bow and quiver.

My arrow, a pen.
You shunned motherhood.
I cannot. But I embrace

your protection,
honed—
a stretched bowstring.

Becoming "I"

...Begins to churn ...
tranquil...

Writhing amoeba
in my mirror—
grey eye-globes, sea creatures
in my mouth—not my face
but the churn that made me
that I make.

Labor... belly...
...settles down

I labor with this curl,
this fish—
belly-buried
large-headed
straining to breathe
against my becoming.

That is why
I cannot say "I"
without tugging at
my voice.
Tell me who I am.

Come close, girls
for day is near...

Touch me, give me
my boundary—
now I feel the edge.

I feel
this edgeless birthing—
near day.

Consuming Tide

I could eat the sea,
far whiter than an egg—
its cold cuisine

frosts with saline
whipped to a froth
around its bouldered rim.

Shells scraped clean
iced in agates
laced with kelp—

what of
my leavings?

Sense of Change

Eros shook my insides
       like a wind
            tumbling
                  down a mountain
      into oak trees.

Can I trust love
      to leave me   unharmed?

A pressure-shift, a chill—
          alert, the wind's cold weight—
                      sudden silence.

I scan your face,
     await the storm.

Ever-Weeping Rock

Leto and Niobe were once dear friends
but their story ends.

Impossible to tell it—the horror—
neglected cries. Niobe's grief

transforms—she becomes
an ever-weeping rock.

Now every mountain stream steals
my breath—

who weeps, and why?

Desert Litany

Neither the honey nor the bee for me.
Let there be no golden excess—
        pregnant comb
        sticky-sweet amber.

Let chamisa and sage
drink the wind—
        storm spasms
        pressure.
Let lizards skitter
        in yawning arroyos
        with ants and armored beetles.
Let rabbit and raven patrol
        the desert grass,
        arid gusts.

And let there be moonlight—
        a flash across the steppe—
moving shadows, mountain backbone—
        certain, stony
        desert foothold.

On Beginning Again

... In springtime

      a breeze

beneath white blossoms

      hidden hint of coming warmth

            the plum tree's black spikes.

False boundary of the body

(Chorus):
In multicolored, honeyed tones
she pleads for Love to come.
Its bitter sorrows she endures,
its endless depths to plumb.

The Space Between

With what eyes?

Chiffon in a breeze-breath
the air we touch, that divides
us—amethyst folds
billow lavender.

I reach for you—
shoreline sand, swelling
toward breakers, retreating.
On your fluid edge, light dances.

Our gazes lock—
a starling flock's ascent—
black contortion
quick collapse.

Pulled close
I feel your warmth.
Our coming, going
a floating wave.

Confrontation

There is no self—
only many selves I own, disown
multi-limbed, many-headed.

My inner layers
hold your shape.
In you, my imprint.

We live face to face.
Knowing by
being known.

False boundary of the body,
a stand of aspen
joined underground.

I greet the self I know inside
you. *Courage*—we stand,
each *person*.

Love Song

You came and I was eager for you.
       You cooled the yearning
       that burned inside.
My insides are quiet.

I protect the place
       where you touch me—
love's cradle
deserted field.

Breath-walls swell, respire
       your seasons—
winter's bite
summer drought.

A place where living
       flows—
here is where I feel
I know.

Intermingled

Love's gift,
having come from the sky,
wrapped round

in a purple cloak—
cool cyan glow
tinged with fever.

Oh, bring me
orange evenings, the sun
and its burn, currents

of kelp and krill. Spare me
love's disfiguring,
its violet trace.

Bird-Sisters

Spring's messenger, wailing nightingale…
Listen to the story.

                                              (Chorus):
                       The wound that only women know
                              with silence is enforced.
                   From peace and sweet tranquility
                             forever she's divorced.

(Philomela the Swallow to her sister, Procne the Nightingale):

Where were the gods when I needed wings to escape
       his stabs, the burning where he entered me, slash
              of my tongue?

My hands spoke. I twirled the spindle down my thigh as you taught me—
       gentle, unlike his touch. Remember how we dyed this skein,
              our madder-soaked hands?

I pulled the warp threads taut like my muscle bands that night,
       stiff against his thrusts. I untangled silken wefts,
              wove with blood colors.

Swallows burst from cliffside nests—bright confetti—
       their birdsong, our twittering squeals—they
              are my sisters now.

                                              (Chorus):
                            Her sister flew into a rage,
                             boiled justice in a stew.
                     She served their son to him as food—
                         the child's death, pain to brew.

(Procne the Nightingale, to her sister, Philomela the Swallow):

The gods stole my hands
when they gave me wings.
Let them try to stop my telling.

Never silent, day or night
I am forever awake—
so too may he be

who slammed his weight against you—
work-sweat, battle-blood—cut out
your tongue. I trusted him.

My hands wove your fingers
through the web, taught you
how to beat the weft.

Your voice, your tapestry
woven tight—I held you
in my hands.

My hands—wingbeats now—
plunged the knife, choked his father
on our son's tender flesh.

The boy's name and yours—
my nighttime cry,
my morning lament.

Eirana, why
Pandion's daughter, the swallow …
me …?

(Chorus):
The deathless gods responded,
wove the women into birds.
Their feathered colors tell a tale
unspeakable in words.

(Eirana, Voice of Peace):

Winter silence, frost-
cracked memories, uneasy
calm.

Sing your rich-hued tones
to me, for your song, too
will be forgotten.

>
> (Chorus):
> In tapestry, in birdsong
> a sister-tale is spun.
> With tinted threads and feathered flight
> their fate they have outrun.

Unwelcome Visitors

*Their frenzy cooled—
they lowered their wings.*
I thought I was
the harpy—
bones of leathery wings
talons, needle-claws
extensions of my hands.

But the swirl cools
by itself.
The black wings close.
What remains
is not fear.

Still, I feel
wind-pressure
from their wingbeats.
Now every gift comes
with a locked trap door.

In Parallel

You will remember…

… the day your horizon disappeared

your throat burning

invisible ants digging tunnels

your blue weighted blanket

the grey stretch every afternoon

how long an hour was

housed in silence …

… but I recall the February chill

how I parted your hair with my eyes
searched for the coral tint
along your cheekbones

the yellow paper umbrellas
I laid on tumbler rims—
apple juice, herbal tea

the muffled click—
your bedroom door-latch—
white barrier

inbreath
when I saw
the scar.

Love Nest

At the bottom—in faint cries—the knowledge—that your beating heart could stop—my hands cannot—conduct its rhythm—that my child's face could lose—its light—my caring cannot—heal her—that cells in my own breast—conspire to take my life—the weight of it—crisp leaves as they fall—silence—then—a rustle—a pecking—a shell crack

    how hope feels—
    blind, wet-feathered
    faint.

Bridge

Unhinged

What wild woman bewitches your mind?

She casts her spell
that uninvited houseguest
who makes her bed

among my ordered thoughts
pushing "please"
and "may I" aside.

Now she is writing
on my walls.
With lipstick.

> (Chorus):
> No invocation to the Muse,
> no mystic incantation.
> She conjures up a goddess-form,
> a gentle incarnation.

Cosmogenesis

    Oh, goddess, *materialize* here,
    graced with beauty!

Unbowed in my standing prayer
    I dare her to appear—warm, fleshly—
        few would risk it.

I pray—the gods are deaf.
But I have learned
more than prayer
    from Sappho:

        Songs create worlds.

She is my sister-song, child-voice,
    my future
        knowing self.

    Be gentle.

I conjure

    the poem,
        my only home—

            that green shoot
            that running water.

A hue this side of dark

(Chorus):
To simple things her song attends,
she listens past the quiet.
The inner patterns of each day
are where her thoughts run riot.

To Sappho

a sheltered place—
depths of water, milk, blood—
this is where I meet you.

Petronia petronia

My wild heart
        tough, slick
        as shoreline gravel—
bare beach,
        cold tide
                the black earth

beneath *swift sparrows*
        swooping
                from cliff-crag nests
        with close-beating wings
                neck-spots of sky-gold—

I hear their clipped calls
to live
        at home
                in the rocks—
eat sorrow,

        fly.

Earthbound

I would not think fit
       to touch the sky.
I hug the earth
       half-hidden—
a mushroom in peaty turf
     anchored
       tree roots.

Everything clings—
woodland's mossy drape
lichens etched in basalt
      walls of fern,
       rainwater slick
       black cliffs.

Iokolpos

I want what I
almost see—

*violets tucked
in hidden folds—*

a hue
this side of dark.

Hunger
sustains me—

not having but wanting—
honey, pistachios

the ripe fig
on too high a branch.

Ground Cover

Finches, strawberry-stained,
escape notice on grey slate.

Yellow cone-beaks crack
black sunflower husks,

leave delicate seed-cups empty
as sunlight breaks.

Precipice

Becoming happens *for not*—
grabbed by its sleeve
on the brink
just before
the mountain path
gives way.

Hope

The persistent Perhaps
suckles the earth,
resolute

water-strong threads,
celery shoots
resisting life's crush.

Waiting river

(Chorus):
Even in the face of death
a yearning rises up
to see the present with new eyes,
to drink its bitter cup.

Thumos

I *thirst* for emptiness,
the well I drink from—
my *thumos*.

If I could, I would slake
this thirst with water—
clear, cold.

But I am a bound thing,
touched on every side.
I reach

for what *I can,* cannot
see—my *face*
reflected.

What Waits for Me

O, Dream from black night, you are pacing
        when Sleep turns me to the sea—haunting shapes
            carved from wind-whipped junipers—
                a lion's paw, a wingless bird.

                    On black basalt flats
                      mussel-encrusted, seething with spray,
        a pounding, like someone crazed
rattling my windows.

Surging wind
        strips the sparkle from ocean crests
                as if peeling back bridal veils
                        from a flooding grey.

                      My vision persists
                unchased by sunlight
        deep into day.
The horizon empty.

Seascape

The waves *do not*
churn gravel with purpose—
neither kind nor cruel—
indifferent.

Water, mollusk, kelp—
a salty slurry tinged
with dead remains—
blurred distinction.

Immersed
in its aqua churn,
no boundaries—
symbiotic brew.

Stalagmos

Concerning my [pain like a] dripping stalagmite...

My bedrock shifts—
        the earth, liquid.
                Am I underground
    beneath an ocean?

Bitter salt drips through
        my rock layers.
                Pain builds
    its chalky mass.

I find my way through shadows,
        stony swords,
                my home
    a nameless river cave.

Unraveled

*I do not know where to run—
in me two ways of thinking*

intertwine—living, dying—
this web of days.

Opposing tensions bind me —
Will, Fate. I am

a garment soon to be cut
from the loom.

In the Air

Earth's fragrance
stony, verdant—
the *ground* resists the fog,
my *anxiety*.

Acheron

> *... but this*
> *pernicious god...*
> *truly I did not love...*
> *now, though, because...*
> *and the cause neither...*
> *nothing much...*

Now that death lurks, I lust—
    a healthy body
    a hush
    a tomorrow

> *having gained... mercy... trembling...*
> *aging skin now... surrounds... flies, chasing...*
> *violets tucked in hidden folds...*

While death chases me
I run after
    this spring's bloom, stars
    in a roiling sky, forgiveness,
    the unwritten poem.

> *I just want to be dead.*

Too much
to take in—
    my mistakes, broken promises,
    the lullaby I should have sung...

I want to end it—
    more than that,
        I want the wanting.

                      Reaching arms,
                willow branches waving—
                    dew glimmers
                    on the lotus leaves.

>   *…Womanly Dawn… golden-armed…*
>   *fate.*

I confront my fate
like dawn—
gold light.

My daughter speaks
womanly

      "I know my truth—
      no mystery."

           Some yearning holds me in its grip… to see …
                 the lotus-covered banks.

.
 .
  .
   .

Waiting river—
    quiet glide
        past my past.

Still Life with Doves

A pair on a fence wire—
airy, as I pass—
they stare

with ebony eyes *of sleep*.
I repeat my listening.
They repeat their silence.

The wind sighs
dandelion seeds *flying*,
tiny white fireworks.

Ivory tails flash—
a flutter
from the fence.

Coda

Cento Duet

my tongue… shattered—
the clear-voiced bird
      flying

                                 fragments
                                          reveal a world—

forever … unowned
you must speak

                                 will my words survive?

autonomy … leaving me behind—
tender sapling… you

                                 I seek the swirling, pull the future in

a trampled hyacinth

                                 our fates, linked

past mourning

                                 soaring inside spangled worlds

violets tucked in hidden folds

                                 your hand stirs air

I look at you
no longer guileless

                                 migrating songbird
                                 coming, going

road-rider, pathfinder

                                 all I can keep—
                                 tangled fragments, unraveling

gathered … with delicate hands

                                 the great wheel turns—
                                 a door…

bewitches

                                 … becomes a pool,
                                 rain-washed

in another time
      someone will remember

                                 you are the river

a thin fire

                                 emerald quiet—
                                        this dawning fireball

Prayer

Say I *wrapped her well
in fine linen*, that I
unwound the sounds
that mapped her—
vowels deep in the throat,
cicada trills.

Meet Sappho

I am not the first to be snagged by Sappho's snare. Popular in her own day, Sappho has captivated audiences ever since. Perhaps it is her aura of mystery. Who was she? What role did she play in her community? Why is so little left of Sappho's writing? Theories abound.

Sappho lived in the late seventh and early sixth centuries BCE during the so-called archaic era, centuries before Greece's classical age. Literary sources about her life are scarce, late, and authored by males. Sappho's poetry remains our best source of information about her but even that presents challenges, since only fragments of her work remain.

The Fragments

Of the 10,000 lines Sappho is thought to have written, only about 650 lines survive, including just one complete poem. We have nothing written in Sappho's own hand. Over hundreds of years, various people recorded her poems on potsherds, papyrus, and parchments. An early edition of her work was compiled in Alexandria during the Ptolemaic period of Greek influence in Egypt (305 – 30 BCE). This edition did not survive. Some papyri containing poems by Sappho were uncovered at Oxyrhynchus (modern El Bahnasa), an Egyptian city southwest of Cairo where large caches of papyri were excavated when Egypt came under British control at the end of the nineteenth century. Because Sappho was reviled by the Christian church for her luscious images and emotional themes, her work may have been destroyed intentionally.

Some of Sappho's poems were partially reconstructed from scraps of papyrus that were torn into strips for cartonnage, a kind of papier-mâché of papyrus or linen, which was used for ancient Egyptian funerary masks and mummy cases. Still more fragments survive because they were quoted by other ancient authors over several centuries, usually in single verses or phrases. Manuscripts have been discovered as recently as 2004 and 2014. Still, only disconnected pieces survive.

A Singer

Sappho wrote lyrics—songs. Classical vase paintings depict Sappho either with a *barbiton* (a bass version of the *kithara*, a kind of lyre that is strummed or plucked) or a scroll, testaments to her elevated status in antiquity as a lyric poet. Her fragments mention many ancient musical instruments: several kinds of lyre (the *barbiton*; the *chelys*, made from a tortoise shell;

and the *kithara*), the harp-like *paktis*, the *aulos* (a flute made of one or two reed pipes), and the *krotala* (castanets). Speculation persists regarding the settings and audiences to whom she sang.

Sappho's poetry is distinctive. She wrote in the Aeolic dialect, a popular version of Greek in its day but less familiar throughout the ancient world once the Attic dialect became standard for Greek literary composition in the first centuries CE. Sappho devised poetic forms and metrical arrangements that suited her Greek dialect and unique subject matter. One of these inventions is the so-called Sapphic stanza, a metered form comprising three lines of equivalent length and a shorter fourth line.

Sappho was called "The Poetess" in antiquity, the implicit counterpart of Homer, known then as "The Poet." A vast body of scholarship has explored Homer's dating and identity and has reached consensus that "Homer" stands for a community of singers who developed a rich, preliterate epic tradition. I use "Homer" to refer to this community and its orally-composed epics. Homer's dates are debated but he likely predated Sappho by at least a century. Homer's epics, the *Iliad* and the *Odyssey*, were well-known and widely sung in Sappho's time. She certainly knew these epic songs of war heroes and their mighty deeds but Sappho sang in a different vein. Her poems arose from everyday life. They draw their beauty from human experience, the natural world, and universal emotions, especially as experienced by women.

A Woman's World
Perhaps the most common question associated with Sappho's biography concerns her sexual orientation, largely because many of her poems extol the beauty and virtues of other women. But besides speaking affectionately, even passionately, about women, Sappho's poems also express love and respect for men and marriage. Sappho sang from Lesbos, a Greek island in the northeast Aegean Sea, from whence we derive the term, "lesbian." In antiquity, however, the reputation of women from Lesbos suggested intense interest and skill in sexual interactions with males, not other females. Like the sources for Sappho's biography, such rumors originated with male outsiders and usually for suspicious reasons. The truth is that we do not know. Undeniably, Sappho wrote from within a woman's world, referring often to mortal women and immortal goddesses. She mentions brothers, bridegrooms, husbands, and fathers but she typically refers to men in terms of their connections with women. In the surviving fragments, Sappho seldom uses the Greek word for a male.

Sappho and Myth

Like most ancient Greek writers, Sappho knew and invoked the myths of her day. Ancient Greek myths are widely known today but the Greek word *muthos* meant something different in Sappho's time from its current, popular connotation as fantasy, falsehood, or untruth. In ancient Greece, both history and myth were understood as reliable sources of information about the past, providing powerful tools to understand and negotiate the present. History offered written stories while myths were transmitted in speech and song. Both history and myth communicated truth, and both existed in multiple, sometimes contradictory, versions. Just as various historical documents can depict the same event differently, orally transmitted myths offer varying explanations of the origin and destiny of things. Sappho's fragments exhibit how myth conveys truth: not by recounting actual events but by expressing the full range of human emotion, motivation, and experience.

Since we have only a fraction of Sappho's body of work, we do not know all the mythical characters and themes her songs invoked. Nevertheless, we cannot help but notice her multiple references to Leto and Artemis in the surviving fragments (see **Ode to Artemis,** fragment 44Aa, and **Ever-Weeping Rock**, fragment 142). Leto was raped and impregnated by Zeus, king of the Olympian gods, because of her extraordinary beauty. Her daughter, Artemis, rejected marriage and childbirth. These mythical stories resonate in Sappho's clear-eyed exploration of the marvelous and tragic dimensions of love, marriage, and childbirth.

Sappho's Prayers

Epic singers typically invite inspiration by invoking a Muse. Their songs were thought to be the Muse's gifts and singers the instruments of divine inspiration. Sappho's lyric fragments also preserve prayers but Sappho does not invoke the Muses. She prays directly to the gods, especially Hera, queen of goddesses, and Aphrodite, goddess of love. Sappho seems to view herself as a competent singer, not an empty vessel waiting to be filled with divine inspiration. Sappho is no mere supplicant. Her prayers exhibit confidence in her poetic art and a consuming desire for her own and others' well-being. Sappho's prayers are conversations. When she entreats Aphrodite, the goddess answers her.

Translation

My poems employ my own translation of Sappho's fragments, using Heather Waddell's *The Digital Sappho* (https://digitalsappho.org/) and other resources. For her text, Waddell relies primarily on David Campbell's *Greek Lyric: Sappho and Alcaeus* in the Loeb Classical Library, vol. 142 (Harvard University, 1982), and Eva-Maria Voigt's *Sappho and Alcaeus* (Polak and van Gennep, 1971), widely regarded as authoritative editions. I refer to Sappho's fragments using the number scheme employed in those editions (other schemes exist). My poems respond to Sappho's prompts. Throughout the book, my words appear in regular type, while Sappho's words (transliterated or translated into English) appear in *italics*.

An art in itself, translation always requires choices. For one thing, scholars must decide which word(s) were written in the first place. This is more difficult than it might seem and always entails guesswork. Even when translators are certain about the words written, they must choose from among a word's many shades of meaning, based on context. But context is difficult to ascertain in a fragmentary text. All of Sappho's fragments, and indeed all texts, admit of a wide range of translation. When my translations reflect adventurous or unconventional renderings, I explain my decisions in the **Notes**.

Singing In Harmony
I feel that I write, not about Sappho, but *with* her. Sappho's images captivate. I relish her lush descriptions of the natural world. I feel at home in her feminine viewpoint on love, longing, and loss. Sappho's work draws me like iron filings to a magnet. Even in her worn and fragmented state, she has delivered me into the practice of poetry. All but obliterated, her songs have never gone silent. I still hear her singing and celebrating life, love, and even death, with timeless vitality.

Notes

Entwined, p. 6
wordweaver, fragment 188: The Greek word *muthoplokon*. Fragment 188 was preserved in *The Dissertations* by Maximus of Tyre, a rhetorician and philosopher who lived in the second century CE. He remarks in passing, "Socrates calls [erotic] love a Sophist; Sappho, *muthoplokon*." We do not know the context of Sappho's usage.

The Greek word *muthoplokon* is a compound of *muthos* and the noun form of the Greek verb *pleko*. *Muthos* is usually rendered into English as "myth," a misleading translation. In antiquity, myth was paired with history, another Greek word. The difference between the two had to do with their modes of transmission. History denoted a written source about the past, whereas myth denoted a traditional, spoken source. Unlike today, written information in antiquity was not presumed to be more accurate than spoken information. In fact, the ancient world held a long-standing prejudice against written documents as unreliable because their inscribers are absent; documents are disassociated from their writers. Documents can therefore be altered for dishonest purposes, whereas the spoken word, passed down through generations from trusted sources, was considered far more reliable because speaker and hearer remain in contact, face to face.

The verb *pleko* means to twist, coil, or plait. It is the root of the Greek word for weaving, *sympleko*. In the ancient world, weaving and spinning, its necessary preliminary, were pervasive activities. All fabric in the ancient world—clothing, bed linens, tents, sacking, sails on ships—was handwoven on warp-weighted looms with yarn spun by hand using a drop spindle. Spinning and weaving occupied as much time as food preparation until weaving moved into factories early in the Roman imperial period. Even then, spinning and weaving remained manual; they were not mechanized in the West until the Renaissance. Greek goddesses (eg., Athena, Aphrodite) and Homeric characters (eg., Penelope, Helen, Calypso, Circe) were depicted as weavers because skill in textile production met basic social needs. As women's work until these crafts were commercialized, spinning and weaving became symbols of the feminine ideal. The first Roman emperor, Caesar Augustus, made a show of wearing homespun garments to display the industry and virtue of his wife, Livia.

The words for weaving in Greek (*sympleko*) and Latin (*texo*) also served as primary symbols of literature in antiquity. Greek literary critics in the

Hellenistic period referred to literary compositions as *symploke*, which means woven cloth. The English words, "textile" and "text" derive from the Latin verb *texo*, which means to weave. From antiquity until the industrial revolution, spinning and weaving functioned as rich and powerful metaphors for verbal art and, by extension, all kinds of artistic creation. See the notes for **Bird-Sisters** and fragments 135, 136 for an example of weaving as a figure for language.

Ode to Artemis, p. 10
Fragment 44Aa: Sappho's authorship of this fragment is probable but debated.

unowned: The Greek word *parthenos*. This word is usually translated "virgin," a misleading translation. The Greek word refers to a young girl who has not been claimed by a male for marriage. The emphasis of *parthenos* lies in the fact that a girl's father has not yet given her to another male, rather than on the girl's sexual experience. Fragment 44Aa relates Artemis's refusal to be owned by anyone and describes her habitat in the mountains as *oiopolos*, which means lonely or solitary.

by your head: In Fragment 44Aa, Sappho recounts Artemis's confrontation with her father, Zeus, king of the Olympian gods. In that meeting, Artemis declares her independence and pledges to live a solitary life in the mountains. Zeus does not speak but he accedes to her demands with a nod of the head.

unbroken: The Greek word *admes* is usually translated "unwed" or "unmarried" when applied to a woman but its root sense derives from animal training where it means unbroken, in the sense of an untamed animal. Because Artemis declares in fragment 44Aa that she intends to live alone in the mountains among wild animals, I have translated *admes* in **Ode to Artemis** according to its root sense, as "unbroken."

hunting: Artemis the moon goddess was associated with typically masculine activities, such as archery and hunting. She was also revered as the protector of woman's life transitions, especially childbirth and a girl's entry into marriage from childhood (girls married young then). Apollo, god of the sun and twin brother of Artemis, was associated with typically feminine arts of healing, prophecy, care of children, and the love of music and poetry. Both Artemis and Apollo hunted with bow and arrow (See the note on **Ever-Weeping Rock**, fragment 142). Artemis's arrow was thought to bring merciful, painless death.

Becoming "I," p. 11
labor, fragment 43: The Greek word *kamatos*. The word is typically glossed as "toil" or "trouble," sometimes referring to weariness or other outcomes of toil or trouble. Sophocles (c. 497/6—406/5 BCE) uses the word in *Oedipus Rex* (174) to refer to the pangs of childbirth. This meaning makes sense in Fragment 43. The next word in the fragment is *phren*, a word usually translated vaguely as "mind" or "heart" but its Greek sense is less abstract, more visceral, and located in the gut or the center of the torso (see **Love Song**, fragment 48). I translate *phren* in fragment 43 as "belly." The context of childbirth makes sense of this fragment that is notoriously difficult to render into English.

Sense of Change, p. 13
Fragment 47:
Eros, Son of Aphrodite, god of sexual love and the source of the English word, "erotic." The Greek and English languages reflect their culture's different notions of romantic love. Contemporary imagination focuses on pleasurable erotic passion, whereas ancient Greek language and culture imagined Eros as violent and disruptive. In fragments 44Aa and 130, Sappho refers to Eros as the "Loosener of Limbs," using the Greek word *lusimeles*, which also describes the effects of drunkenness and sleep.

inside(s): The Greek word *phren* names what is shaken in fragment 47. It is often translated "heart" or "mind" because its Greek sense refers to the place in the body where thought and feeling reside. Modern English distinguishes sharply between thought and feeling, often opposing the head and heart as locations of conflicting processes. This opposition is alien to the Greek idea that thoughts and feelings arise together from internal organs in the torso. I translate *phren* as "belly" in fragment **Becoming "I"** (fragment 43) and as "inside(s)" in **Sense of Change** (fragment 47) and **Love Song** (fragments 48 and 120).

Ever-Weeping Rock, p. 14
Leto, Niobe, fragment 142: In Greek myth, Leto, daughter of the Titans Coeus and Phoebe, was raped and impregnated by Zeus, king of the

Olympian gods. Zeus's wife and queen, Hera, jealously pursued Leto during her pregnancy. Leto fled, searching for a safe place to give birth, settling finally on the island of Delos. After a long and difficult labor there, she gave birth to twins: Artemis, goddess of the moon, and (nine days later) Apollo, god of the sun. Both Artemis and Apollo were skilled in the use of bow and arrow.

Niobe was a wealthy woman, the daughter of Tantalus and wife of Amphion of Thebes. According to Greek myth, she bore many children (six of each sex according to Homer, seven of each sex according to Ovid). Out of pride over her large and wealthy family, she boasted to her friend, Leto, and claimed superiority over her. Because Leto's life had been shaped by difficulty with conception, pregnancy, and childbirth, she became jealous of Niobe. Leto sent her own children, Artemis and Apollo, to kill all of Niobe's children with bow and arrow. After their murders, the gods buried the corpses. In her sorrow, Niobe was transformed into a rock covered with running water, memorializing the tears that forever flowed down her face after the murder of her children.

Love Song, p. 21
insides, fragment 120: See note on *inside(s)* in fragment 48, for **Sense of Change.**

Intermingled, p. 22
purple cloak, fragment 54: One of Sappho's favorite colors is purple, a royal color because the dyestuff used to make purple was difficult to obtain in antiquity and therefore expensive to produce. Purple is a mixed color (red and blue) that sometimes symbolizes sadness. Fragment 54 mentions love's arrival from the sky, a likely reference to Aphrodite, the goddess of love. Her purple cloak suggests Sappho's understanding of love, which includes both intense joy and deep sorrow. See **Love Song** and fragment 48 for another example of Sappho's sense of love as a mixture of opposites.

Bird-Sisters, pp. 23-24
Fragments 135, 136:
Swallow (fragment 135), *nightingale* (fragment 136): The cliff swallow is said to be the most popular bird in Greece, where people welcome large flocks of cliff swallows each year as harbingers of spring. The common

nightingale is an Old-World flycatcher with plain, brown markings. It ranges across southern Europe, central Asia, and central China and migrates to sub-Saharan Africa in winter. The nightingale is known for its powerful and varied song, which it sings day and night. The strength and complexity of its song accounts for why western literature often interprets the nightingale as a symbol for poetry and other artistic creation.

Fragments 135 and 136 refer to the ancient myth of Philomela and Procne. Homer's *Odyssey* is the earliest source for this ancient Greek tale that recurs in the classical period in a lost play by Sophocles (*Tereus*), then in the Roman imperial period with (Pseudo-)Apollodorus (*The Library*). Ovid's Latin version of the tale in his *Metamorphoses* likely served as a source for Shakespeare's *Titus Andronicus*. The riveting story of Philomela and Procne remains as poignant today as it was in antiquity.

Pandion, Legendary king of Athens, fathered two daughters, Philomela and Procne. Procne's husband raped Philomela, then cut out her tongue to prevent her from reporting the assault. Determined to tell her story, Philomela wove a figural, multi-colored tapestry depicting the attack. She gave the cloth to her sister, Procne, who became enraged. To avenge her sister's violation, Procne killed the son she had borne with her husband, Philomela's attacker, then served the boy to his father to eat. Outcry over the scene's horrific violence reached the gods, who transformed all three characters into birds to save the women from the rapist's fury. Procne's husband became a hoopoe, a bird known by its crest that looks like a crown. Philomela became a swallow and Procne became a nightingale. In some versions of the story, Philomela became a nightingale and Procne became a swallow.

Eirana (fragment 135): An English transliteration of the Greek word for peace or tranquility. It is sometimes thought to name an unknown, historical woman in fragment 135 but the word is also sensible here as the personification of peace and tranquility, just as Sappho elsewhere personifies Dawn (**Someone Else's Earth,** fragment 123; **Acheron,** fragments 6), Evening (fragment 104A), and Dream (**What Waits for Me,** fragment 63).

Unwelcome Visitors, p. 26
wings, fragment 42: This fragment does not specify a particular kind of winged entity but the frenzy Sappho mentions in fragment 42 evokes the

idea of a harpy. In the Greek mythical imagination, harpies are half-human bird-like creatures who personify the storm winds. Hesiod (a Greek poet active between the late eighth and early seventh centuries BCE and Homer's contemporary) describes the harpy's human dimension in terms of female beauty. But the classical Greek playwright Aeschylus (525-456 BCE) imagines harpies as ugly, violent, and terrifying. They were thought to steal food from their victims and sometimes even to carry the victims away in their talons.

thumos: See the note on *thirst*, fragment 4, for **Thumos**. In **Unwelcome Visitors**, I translate *thumos* as "frenzy."

Cosmogenesis, p. 32

pray, fragment 17: Some of Sappho's fragments preserve prayers, usually to goddesses. Sappho addresses fragment 17 to Hera, Queen of the Olympian gods and goddess of hearth and home. In this prayer she mentions the sons of Atreus, Agamemnon and Menelaus. Agamemnon was the king of Mycenae whose quarrel with Achilles shaped the plot of Homer's *Iliad*. Menelaus, his brother, was the king of Sparta whose wife, Helen, fled Sparta with Paris to Troy, provoking the Trojan war. In fragment 17, Sappho notes that these ancient heroes could wage war and win but could not manage to find their way home without Hera's help. Sappho argues that since Hera answered their prayers, she should also grant Sappho's petition.

Petronia petronia, p. 36

Fragment 1:

swift sparrows: Sappho addresses fragment 1 to Aphrodite, goddess of love and daughter of Zeus, king of the Olympian gods and god of the sky. In this fragment Sappho mentions his golden house, where, according to myth, even the walls are made of gold. Sappho envisions Aphrodite's arrival in the form of a flock of sparrows. The rock sparrow is native to Greece in a range from Spain to central China. Its scientific name, *Petronia petronia*, derives from the Greek word for rock. Rock sparrows nest in crevices and can be found swooping down mountain sides. Both males and females show a yellow spot on the throat.

black earth: Sappho frequently refers to the ground as the black earth. Epic and lyric poets employ epithets or stock phrases to imply rich associations for gods, people, and natural phenomena. For example, Homer's epics famously refer to his heroes' adventures on "the wine-dark sea," implying an intoxicating effect of sea adventure. By contrast, Sappho's epithet "black earth" reflects her earthbound context and suggests the soil's fertility and fecundity.

Iokolpos, p. 38

iokolpos, fragments 21, 30, 58-59, 103: A compound Greek word that combines *ion* (violet) and *kolpos* (multiple meanings). Translations vary according to the translator's construal of *kolpos*, whose semantic field encompasses various kinds of folds or cleavage. It can mean the cleavage between the breasts, the folds of a garment, a cave, a valley, a winding coastline, any depression or cavity, or the vagina. Authoritative lexica of classical Greek list Sappho's uses of *iokolpos* as their only examples, suggesting that Sappho might have invented the word. *Iokolpos* occurs in extant Sappho fragments five times, describing a woman in flight (fragment 21), a bride (fragment 30, two occurrences in fragment 103,) and the Muses (fragments 58-59). Sappho's translators stumble. Most translations refer to being wrapped in a purple robe or cloak. More literally but perhaps euphemistically, Stanley Lombardo (*Sappho: Poems and Fragments*. Indianapolis: Hackett, 2002) gives "violet-breasted," while Anne Carson (*If Not, Winter: Fragments of Sappho*. New York: Vintage Books, 2002) has "violets in her lap." I translate *iokolpos* as "violets tucked in hidden folds" in **Iokolpos, Acheron** (fragment 21), and in **Cento Duet.**

Thumos, p. 45

thirst, fragment 4: The Greek word *thumos*. This Greek word persists in English as "enthusiasm." *Thumos* is difficult to translate because it represents one of the many ways Greek thinking differs from modern ideas expressed in English. In Greek, *thumos* can refer to many things, all related to vitality, powerful feelings, and deep thought. It is often translated "spirit," "soul," "breath," "desire," "mind," or "heart," abstract concepts in English. Sappho's use of *thumos* is anything but abstract, describing visceral, embodied experiences. In the first line of **Thumos**, I translate *thumos* as "thirst." See **Unwelcome Visitors**, fragment 42, where I translate it as "frenzy."

Stalagmos, p. 48

stalagmos, fragment 37: This fragment consists of two unrelated quotations from Sappho in a mid-ninth century encyclopedia of etymology (the history of words). The handbook's author quotes Sappho in his discussion of the Greek word *stalagmos*, which means dripping or dropping. The handbook's example from Sappho consists of just three words. Translated literally, they read, "concerning my dripping," an odd phrase. But the handbook author explains that the Aeolians, an ancient Greek tribe in whose dialect Sappho wrote, used *stalagmos* to refer to pain. I have taken a liberty in translating *stalagmos* in this fragment as "*[pain like a] dripping stalagmite.*"

Acheron, pp. 51-52
violets tucked in hidden folds, fragment 21: See the note for **Iokolpos**.

Dawn: A personification of the natural phenomenon. See the note about personification on *Eirana* for **Bird-Sisters.**

yearning, fragment 95: The yearning Sappho mentions in fragment 95 is for the Acheron, an actual river in northwestern Greece that flows west and drains into the Ionian Sea. In ancient times it took on a mythic dimension associated with death, doom, and foreboding. In Homer's *Odyssey,* the Acheron was one of the rivers of Hades, the land of the dead, where Odysseus consulted "shades" of the dead who could watch but not affect living people and current events. Herodotus (484-425 BCE), historian of the Greco-Persian Wars, cites the Acheron as the location of a death oracle. In fragment 95 Sappho adopts a more receptive posture toward death in her longing for the Acheron's "dewy, lotus-covered banks."

Cento Duet, p. 57
unowned, fragment 44aA: See the note for **Ode to Artemis.**

violets tucked in hidden folds: See the note for **Iokolpos**.

Prayer, p. 58
wrapped, fragment 100: Some of Sappho's fragments were preserved accidentally because the papyrus on which they were written was later torn into strips for cartonnage, a kind of papier-mâché technique used to make mummy cases and funerary masks.

cicada: ancient Greek literature bursts with pride over the beauty of its sounds. Many writers compare Greek speech sounds to the buzzing of cicada wings, a sound they loved.

Fragment Index
In the order the poems appear
in *Sappho Prompts*

Fragment numbers in **bold face** indicate that the designated poem contains the entire fragment.

Water Song for Sappho 118
Someone Else's Earth 2, **12**, 34, **123**
Entwined **188**
Unbounded **125**
Ode to Artemis 44Aa
Becoming "I" **43**
Consuming Tide **167**
Sense of Change **47**
Ever-Weeping Rock **142**
Desert Litany **146**
On Beginning Again 2
The Space Between **162**
Confrontation 24C
Love Song **48,** 120
Intermingled **54**
Bird-Sisters **135, 136**
Unwelcome Visitors **42**
In Parallel 24A
Love Nest **24D**
Unhinged 57
Cosmogenesis 17
To Sappho **29A**
Petronia petronia 1
Earthbound **52**
Iokolpos 21, 30, 58-59, 103
Ground Cover **25**
Precipice **61**
Hope **191**
Thumos 4
What Waits for Me 63
Seascape **145**
Stalagmos 37
Unraveled **51**
In the Air **87B**

Acheron 6, 21, **67a**, 94, 95
Still Life with Doves **97**
Cento Duet 5, 21, 30, 31, 44Aa, 57, 62, 68a, 81, 105b, 114, 115, 118, 147
Prayer **100**

Fragment Index
In alphabetical order by poem title

Fragment numbers in **bold face** indicate that the designated poem contains the entire fragment.

Acheron 6, 21, **67a**, 94, 95
Bird-Sisters **135, 136**
Becoming "I" **43**
Cento Duet 5, 21, 30, 31, 44Aa, 57, 62, 68a, 81, 105b, 114, 115, 118, 147
Confrontation **24C**
Consuming Tide **167**
Cosmogenesis 17
Desert Litany **146**
Earthbound **52**
Entwined **188**
Ever-Weeping Rock **142**
In Parallel 24A
Ground Cover **25**
Hope **191**
In the Air **87B**
Intermingled **54**
Love Song **48**, 120
Iokolpos 21, 30, 58-59, 103
Love Nest **24D**
Ode to Artemis 44Aa
On Beginning Again 2
Petronia petronia 1
Prayer **100**
Precipice **61**
Seascape **145**
Sense of Change **47**
Someone Else's Earth 2, **12**, 34, **123**
Stalagmos 37
Still Life with Doves **97**
Unbounded **125**
Unhinged 57
Unraveled **51**
The Space Between **162**
Thumos 4

To Sappho **29A**
Unwelcome Visitors **42**
What Waits for Me 63
Water Song for Sappho 118

Artist's Statement

"Voices"
Watercolor and ink on Khadi paper

To create this image, I closed my eyes and traced the contours of my face while drawing those curves in black lines. Then I added watercolor, using ultramarine to express depth of feeling and to suggest the sea that surrounds Sappho's island. I used burnt sienna for the richness of the earth that Sappho loved and aureolin for the never-dying light that Sappho glimpsed, applying the paint wet-in-wet to blend shades of grey, green, and gold. The resulting overlapping portraits echo the verbal mixing that infused my translation, reading, and writing of this book. My commentators on this manuscript urged me throughout my writing process to disentangle my voice from Sappho's but I could not. In coming to terms with the Greek fragments, rendering Sappho's words into English, and attaching my words to the upwelling of emotion those ancient songs aroused, I heard only polyphony, never plainsong. I hope this image evokes the voices that reverberate through time in my poems.

Acknowledgments

Anne Carson's brilliant translation of Sappho, *If Not, Winter: Fragments of Sappho* (Vintage 2003) first inspired my exploration of Sappho's fragments and my entry into poetry. Dr. Carson graciously encouraged this project. Brandon Scott, my life partner, urged me to immerse myself in Sappho's work and to translate her entire corpus. Susan Kay Anderson, author of *Mezzanine* (Finishing Line 2019), suggested that I expand my first chapbook, *Someone Else's Earth* (Finishing Line 2021), into this full-length work. James Gaynor, author of *I'll Miss You Later* (Pinfeather 2021) and *Breaking Up on X: Poems for a Nation in Crisis* (Pinfeather 2025), charged the project with enthusiasm at a low point and went on his way rejoicing. Catherine Strisik, author of *Thousand Cricket Song* (Plain View, 2010, 2016), *The Mistress* (3: A Taos Press 2016), *Insectum Gravitis* (Main Street Rag 2019), and *Goat, Goddess, Moon* (Holy Cow! 2025) read the manuscript and offered many helpful suggestions. Judith Chibante Neal, author of *Radio in the Night* (Finishing Line 2017), critiqued multiple versions of several poems. Jock Jacober inspired a late revision of the book. I owe special thanks to Veronica Golos, author of *A Bell Buried Deep* (Story Line 2003), *Vocabulary of Silence* (Red Hen 2011), *Rootwork* (3: A Taos Press 2015), and *Girl* (3: A Taos Press 2019) and to Aubrey Green, managing editor of *eMerge Magazine,* for their endorsements. Veronica Golos suggested the title of this book and edited the manuscript line by line with passion and brilliance. I am a different poet because of her and, I hope, a better one.

An earlier version of **Iokolpos** appeared the *Atlanta Review* in its 2023 Fall/Winter issue as a finalist in their annual International Poetry Contest. The following poems appear in my chapbook, *Orange Persephone* (Finishing Line 2025), with some changes and without the epigraphs from Sappho: "Acheron," "Becoming 'I,'" "Confrontation," "Love Nest," "Ode to Artemis," "Unraveled," "You Will Remember." Earlier versions of some poems appear, many with different titles, in my debut poetry collection, *Someone Else's Earth* (Finishing Line 2021). "Desert Litany" revises "Into the Desert" from my chapbook, *Sagebrush Songs* (Finishing Line 2022).

Margaret Lee is a poet, scholar, fiber artist, watercolor sketcher, and aspiring naturalist in Tulsa, Oklahoma. She finds poems in the Oklahoma prairies, New Mexico deserts, Oregon seashores, and inner landscapes. Her previous chapbooks with Finishing Line Press include *Someone Else's Earth* (2021), which builds poems around surviving fragments of Sappho; *Sagebrush Songs* (2022), a meditation on landscapes of northern New Mexico; *Oklahoma Summer* (2023), which reflects on recent ecological and demographic challenges in Oklahoma, and *Orange Persephone* (2025), a journey through personal crisis. Her poems have also appeared in *From Behind the Mask,* (Paperback-Press 2020), *Echoes of Tradition: Indigenous Orientation to Community, Time, and Land* (Tulsa NightWriters 2024), *The Atlanta Review* and *Pangyrus*. Her book reviews appear in the *Taos Journal of Poetry* and *The Compulsive Reader*. Margaret earned a B.A. in History from Seattle University, Seattle, WA; an M.Div. from Phillips Theological Seminary, Tulsa, OK; and a Th.D. from the Melbourne College of Divinity, Melbourne, Australia. Her academic research and publications focus on the ancient Greek language and the history and culture of the ancient world.

www.ingramcontent.com/pod-product-compliance
Lightning Source LLC
Chambersburg PA
CBHW030056170426
43197CB00010B/1543